A CIRCLE OF NATIONS

VOICES AND VISIONS

OF AMERICAN INDIANS

**NORTH AMERICAN NATIVE
WRITERS & PHOTOGRAPHERS**

FOREWORD BY
Leslie Marmon Silko

INTRODUCTION BY
Michael Dorris

EDITED BY
John Gattuso

BEYOND WORDS PUBLISHING, INC.

To Carla, whose love sustains us
John Gattuso

PUBLISHER

Beyond Words Publishing, Inc.

13950 NW Pumpkin Ridge Road

Hillsboro, Oregon 97124

503-647-5109

DESIGN

Jim Lommasson

and Mary Ann W. Puls

PREPRESS PRODUCTION

Exact Imaging, Inc.

PRINTING

The Irwin-Hodson Company

BINDING

Lincoln & Allen Bindery

THE EARTHSONG COLLECTION

Books that plant trees, save eagles,

and celebrate life on Earth

Light on the Land

Moloka'i: An Island in Time

Keepers of the Spirit

Quiet Pride

The American Eagle

Wisdomkeepers

Within a Rainbowed Sea

"The Indian with a Camera" excerpted from
Videomakers and Basketmakers. Copyright © 1990 by
Leslie Marmon Silko. Reprinted by permission from
Cultures in Transition, *Aperture*, New York.

"The Kaw River Rushes Westward" excerpted from
*Sáanii Dahataał, The Women Are Singing: Poems and
Stories*, Sun Tracks, Volume 23. Copyright © 1993 by
Luci Tapahonso. Reprinted by permission of the University
of Arizona Press.

Library of Congress Cataloging-in-Publication Data

A Circle of nations : voices and visions of American
    Indians / North American Native writers & photographers ;
    edited by John Gattuso ; foreword by Leslie Marmon Silko.
        p.   cm.
    ISBN 0-941831-90-6 : $39.95
        1. Indians of North America—Social life and customs.
    2. Indians of North America—Writing.
    3. Indian literature. 4. Indians of North America—
    Pictorial works. I. Gattuso, John.
    E98.S7C57   1993
    973´.00497—dc20   93-4516
                                                   CIP

Printed in the United States of America.
This book is printed on recycled paper.
Distributed to the book trade by Publishers Group West.

TABLE OF CONTENTS

THE INDIAN WITH A CAMERA

Leslie Marmon Silko

Petroglyphs on rock outcrops along the San Jose River suggest that the Paleo-Indian ancestors of the Pueblos had already begun to make images of spiritual significance on the sandstone 18,000 years ago. Pueblo kivas have stylized abstract designs painted on the walls and altarpieces. The Pueblo people had long understood that certain man-made visual images were sacred and were necessary to Pueblo ceremony. **T**he Pueblo people did not fear or hate cameras or the photographic image so much as they objected to the intrusive vulgarity of the white men who gazed through the lens. My grandfather, Henry Marmon, attended Indian school in Riverside, California, which might explain his fascination with and purchase of a snapshot camera in the 1920s. As a child in the 1950s, I remember the delight of bringing out the old Hopi basket with the grasshopperman design, because Grandma Lillie kept all of Grandpa Hank's snapshots and all the other family snapshots in the tall Hopi basket.

My sisters and cousins and I were too young to recognize the old-time people in the photographs, although we often recognized mesas and hills and certain houses. And so it was necessary that any viewing of the old snapshots in the Hopi basket be accompanied by a running commentary by my father and Grandma Lillie, although they sometimes had to ask Grandpa Hank to help identify the really old Laguna people long dead and gone. The identification of the faces and the places in the photographs never failed to precipitate wonderful stories about the "old days," which in turn brought out even older stories that stretched far beyond the confines of the snapshots in the grasshopper basket.

Our family is of mixed Laguna and white ancestry, but as a child I saw that many of the homes of the most traditional and conservative Laguna people included a great many photographs of family members.

At first, white men and their cameras were not barred from the sacred katchina dances and kiva rites. But soon the Hopis and other Pueblo people learned from experience that most white photographers attending sacred dances were cheap voyeurs who had no reverence for the spiritual. Worse, Pueblo leaders feared the photographs would be used to prosecute the caciques and other kiva members, because the United States government had outlawed the practice of the Pueblo religion in favor of Christianity exclusively.

Pueblo people may not believe that the camera steals the soul of the subject, but certainly the Pueblo people are quite aware of the intimate nature of the photographic image. Because Pueblo people appreciate so deeply the power and significance of the photographic image, they refuse to allow strangers with cameras the outrages to privacy that had been forced upon Pueblo people in the past.

Pueblo people may not believe that the camera steals the soul of the subject, but certainly the Pueblo people are quite aware of the intimate nature of the photographic image.

5

Hopi, Aztec, Maya, Inca—
these are the people who
would not die, the people
who do not change because
they are always changing.
The Indian with a camera
announces the twilight of
Eurocentric America.

Pueblo cultures seek to include rather than exclude. The Pueblo impulse is to accept and incorporate what works, because human survival in the Southwestern climate is so arduous and risky. Before the Europeans appeared, the cultures of the Americas had vast networks of trade and commerce; during times of famine, trade partners sent food. Guatemalan macaw feathers went to Taos, and Minnesota pipestones to Honduras.

Europeans were shocked at the speed and ease with which Native Americans synthesized, then incorporated, what was alien and new. Mexican Indians had embraced Jesus, Mary, Joseph, and the saints almost at once; the Indians had happily set the Christian gods on their altars to join the legions of older American spirits and gods. The Europeans completely misread the inclusivity of the Native American worldview, and they were disgusted by what they perceived to be weakness and disloyalty by the Indians to their Indian gods. For Europeans, it was quite unimaginable that Quetzalcoatl might ever share the altar with Jesus.

Euro-Americans project their own fears and values in their perception of a "conflict" between Native American photographers and traditional Native artists. Traditional artists reassure the Euro-Americans that, while not extinct, Native Americans are not truly part of American society. The Indian with a camera is frightening for a number of reasons. Euro-Americans desperately need to believe that the indigenous people and cultures which were destroyed were somehow less than human; Indian photographers are proof to the contrary.

The Indian with a camera is an omen of a time in the future that all Euro-Americans unconsciously dread: the time when the indigenous people of the Americas will retake their land. Euro-Americans distract themselves with whether a "real" or "traditional" or "authentic" Indian would, should, or could work with a camera. (Get those Indians back to their basket-making!)

Euro-Americans desperately try to deny what has already begun, that inexorable force which has already been set loose in the Americas. Hopi, Aztec, Maya, Inca—these are the people who would not die, the people who do not change, because they are always changing. The Indian with a camera announces the twilight of Eurocentric America.

Pueblo people today are quite sophisticated about film and video technology. Like all human beings they are concerned with their continued survival as the people *they believe themselves to be*. What is essential to all Pueblo people is that generation after generation will continue to remember and to tell one another who they are, who they have been, and who they may become.

Pueblo narratives are not mere bedtime stories or light entertainment. Through the narratives Pueblo people have for thousands of years maintained and transmitted their entire culture; all the strategies and beliefs necessary to Pueblo survival are not written, but they are remembered and repeated generation after generation. Even the most ordinary deer-hunting story is dense with information, from stalking techniques to weather forecasting and the correct rituals to be performed in honor of the dead deer. In short, the stories and reminiscences that enliven all Pueblo social gatherings are densely encoded with expression and information.

When the United States government began to forcibly remove Pueblo children to distant boarding schools in the 1890s, the Pueblo people faced a great crisis. Like the slaughter of the buffalo, the removal of Native American children to boarding schools was a calculated act of cultural genocide. How would the children hear and see, how would the children learn and remember what Pueblo people, what Native Americans for thousands of years had known and remembered together?

But the calculations failed. Eventually the children were returned to their beloved sandstone and expanses of blue sky; again the place soaked them in, and they were reunited with what continues and what has always continued.

Michael Dorris

The essays and photographs in this book have in common a remarkable particularity of vision. Experiences—visual and historical—are captured in their full specificity. Each moment is complete unto itself, distinct from any other, populated by elements and people as real as a brick of clay. These are words and pictures with personality, the result of self-conscious, subjective examination and choice. They resonate with the tension of individual response and record the eye and the ear of their creators like bold artistic fingerprints. There's nothing ephemeral here, nothing tentative. "This happened," essay after essay asserts. "This was how it was the day I saw it," the images announce.

This very lack of apology or qualification imparts an aura of power to these family stories. Personal anecdotes are treated as important data. Incident signifies and gives meaning. It matters who said what, when, and to whom. It's telling what a person wears, how he or she stands. Actions shape and bind context the way mesas rise out of flat land. Events are grounded in every sense of the word.

"The energy crackled," Creek poet and musician Joy Harjo says of her coming of age at the Institute of American Indian Arts among other young people from many tribes, "the same kind of energy needed to shift continental plates, to propel a child into the world to start all over again."

"I knew that blood could talk," Harjo goes on to state, a conviction marvelously shared by Simon Ortiz as he recounts the events thirty years ago that affirmed his decision to write. "It seemed that stories, especially the stories that come out of the oral tradition, offered explanations of just about everything," he says. "They held the narrative power of the mythic, a power that calls all things into existence and assures respect for life all around."

Linda Hogan remembers her Chickasaw grandmother as "the beautiful lover of land, people, and quiet Oklahoma nights full of remembered fear, wet heavy air, fireflies, and the smell of pecan trees, the land with tarantulas and rattlesnakes, the numerous and silencing sounds of gunshots in the night." This wedding of emotion and sensation, grace and excitement, place and impression into a single, solid recollection is vivid and startling, complete as an unexpected view from the top of a high hill.

"The air is crowded with words," announces Debra CallingThunder, born of a Sky People renowned as devotees and prophets who continuously see signs and wonders, "wondrous and beautiful words that rise invisible and unheard and then are swallowed by time." But they are not altogether lost, if organized into stories and songs. The pictures preserved can be awful, terrible as well as lovely—such is their mission to instruct, to remind, to heal.

Mark Trahant, a mixed-blood Shoshone-Bannock, considers the power of the single term *Indian* to define, either by exclusion or inclusion, and he discovers through this exercise a means by which finally to identify himself.

Paula Gunn Allen, novelist, poet, and critic, draws a circle of her travels between New Mexico and California and concludes that "going always brings return." "At Mother's death," she writes, "I returned, an aging and grieving woman. Mother wasn't there, only the wind, mysterious in its soughing; only faded memories, great, gaunt vistas, November light, and cold, cold wind. You can see the entire little village from the Chair; you can see eons of Earth's life; you can see millennia of all that is past and returns no more. My mother climbed those mesas in her youth, like her daughter, like her daughter's daughter, like our sons."

Memory and anticipation, past and future, border the present like the two shores of a river, like the land beneath Elizabeth Woody's childhood house and the sky above it. "The geography of our landscape—the snowcapped Cascade range of volcanoes, surrounded by evergreen forests and high desert—is an integral element of the culture of the Plateau, as we are collectively called. I belong to a people who cherished the land." And who listened to it. "In the sound of water, the sheen of river stone, a song is pervasive and faithful to continuance, the memory in its own language tells the story well."

Luci Tapahonso also finds a place of refuge and renewal in the embrace of her acutely observed tribal home. "We drove into the yard late at night," she begins her description, "and my parents were awake, waiting for us. After we ate a long-awaited meal of mutton stew and *náneeskaadí* (tortillas), we went to bed. It was dark and quiet in the house of my childhood. My daughter and I talked quietly a while before we fell asleep. In the darkness, we heard the faint songs of the Yeis, the grandfathers of the holy people, and the low, even rhythm of the drum. They had been dancing and singing for six days and nights already. From across the river valley, the songs drifted into our last waking moments, into our dreams. While we slept, they sang, praying and giving thanks for the harvest, for our return and the hundreds of others who returned home that weekend for the fall festivities. The Yeis danced for all of us—they danced in their fatigue, they danced in our tired dreams. They sang for us until their voices were hardly more than a whisper."

White Deer of Autumn's essay centers on a quest for vision. He seeks not sight in the simplest sense, but a view that's introspective and whole, a vision that comes only when a person is ready to receive it. Finally it comes.

"The vision I received that night under the stars at Powderhorn Park, a thousand miles from the island where I first cried for one, became the guiding force and anchor of my life," he tells us. "Whenever I need to know whether or not I am doing the right thing for the People and the land, I recall my vision.... It has kept me on the path of heart. It is the one thing that I know can never be taken away from me."

Coursing through these memoirs and contemplations, these striking and diverse photographs, enlivening them as with a common blood, is the excitement of discovery. New terrains are stumbled upon, old truths are seen in new light, connections become clear, things make sense. A spiritual topography emerges, the self linked back and forth in time and space, the joy of following a well-worn path, at last with some certainty of arriving at the proper destination.

METAMORPHOSIS

Joy Harjo

When I started Indian School in Santa Fe in 1967, I knew I had escaped the emotional winter of my alcoholic childhood home. There was no one to talk to except the invisible world, nothing to move me but the music I heard on the radio—the shout and flame of James Brown, the crooning of the Four Tops, and the brash bands of the English Invasion. There were family stories about Monahwee, my great-great-grandfather, who led the Red Stick War in the early 1800s, one of the largest Indian wars in this country, but as a teenager I had difficulty placing that history on the template of my childhood. And yet those stories of resistance kept my heart beating toward an unknown possibility, a promise of creative change.

It was in the fire and creativity of Indian school, newly renamed the
Institute of American Indian Arts, that my spirit made steps back
from the assaults of childhood, of culture. It was not a solitary journey.
Rather, it was made with a collective of students that included Inuit
from Alaska, Miccosukee from Florida, and many tribes in-between.
Yet we made alliances, or rather they were often made for us accord-
ing to tribal history.

The Siouxs hung together; the Pawnees avoided them. The Pueblos
clung together, as did the Navajos. And then there
were the Washington State Indians who were an active
political force. I belonged to the "Civilized Tribes,"
which included the Creeks, Choctaws, Cherokees,
Chickasaws, and Seminoles. And there were divisions
within the divisions. You were either a cowboy or a
hippie, a freak or a straight. Yet we were all "skins"
traveling together in an age of metamorphosis, many

of us facing the same tests of rage, locked grief, alienation. History
still talked to us, still lived, and we were direct evidence of the struggles of our great-grandparents, though many of us wore bell-bottoms
and Lennon glasses and listened to the psychedelic music of the
exploding times. We felt united.

In the Civilized Tribes, some of us were considered black because of
intermarriages and alliances with African-Americans. A Choctaw
student who was a fine piano player and a sweet gentleman was
obviously part black and sometimes excluded for that reason. I, too,
despite my light skin, was teased because of my family's black history.

Then Danny sprang by, lit up with a fierce anger. We were all surprised as he leapt brutally onto the hoods of every car in the administration parking lot, crushing them one by one. There was no mercy. But this didn't satisfy his anger, an anger larger than the tall cottonwoods watching our intense human drama. He grew with the anger and kicked in each set of windows lining the academic building. Around him a whirling halo glowed a brownish red. Within the whirl were racial epithets, his baby-self abandoned by his mother for a drink, the running-away ghost of his father. Two teachers grabbed him and threw him to the ground. Tears ran from me, tears made of the same anger.

Years later, as I drove up on his reservation in South Dakota, I was nearly knocked down by the force of events called power that encircled a land so beautiful you wept. I understood the boy who kicked through a little tear in the fabric so many years ago. The discrepancy between his world of loss and images of horses on the plains could only be met first with anger.

Women often turn their anger inward, and at Indian school it was no different. We manifested it by mutilating ourselves or less often by attacking others. Yet each scar was evidence that we wished to live. We had to keep knives away from one Pueblo student, one of the best painters. We often carried another student to the Indian hospital to have her stomach pumped. She was a stunningly beautiful dancer. We had to hunt down another friend before she froze to death in the snow. She was trying to go home—to a home that was not there. We never really talked about any of this. We did what we could to save each other in the moment.

Just as our bodies were impressed with our anger, they also provided the canvas of our most intimate art. Once some of my roommates decided to tattoo themselves with needles and black ink. I contemplated what I would tattoo on my hands, but I was not in love enough with anyone to tattoo their initials and L-O-V-E on my knuckles as another girl was doing. Besides, it looked like it hurt. It was an initiation of sorts. There was no ice-numbing here. Only a few girls endured it, either for love or as a mark of blood to show their bravery or to note a particular event, a breakup, an accomplishment.

Twenty-five years later when I picked my daughter up from Rehoboth Indian School near Gallup and met the boyfriend who had made her soggy with grief for summer vacation, his hand blazed with her initials. They were still seeping blood. I knew I had trouble.

I marked myself once with a knife. I was disappearing into the adolescent sea of rage and destruction, but the mark of pain assured me of my own reality. The cut could speak. It had a voice that cried out when I could not make a sound in my defense. I knew that blood could talk. It was full of the stories that call us human, that link us with stars as well as the Earth. I thought I did not want to live, yet a shining sound burned at the center of my heart, urging me to stand like a tall cedar pole pointed toward the apex of the starry sky. It rescued me from the oblivion of unknown terrors of memory.

It was the stuff of my generation, we who came of age in that best and worst of times. We broke the surface of memory with stories of our anger and great love. We were mixed rage and beauty. And we moved from that place to remake the world in our image.

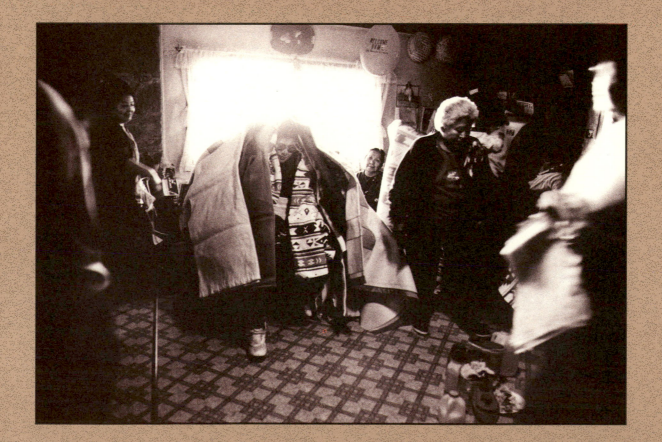

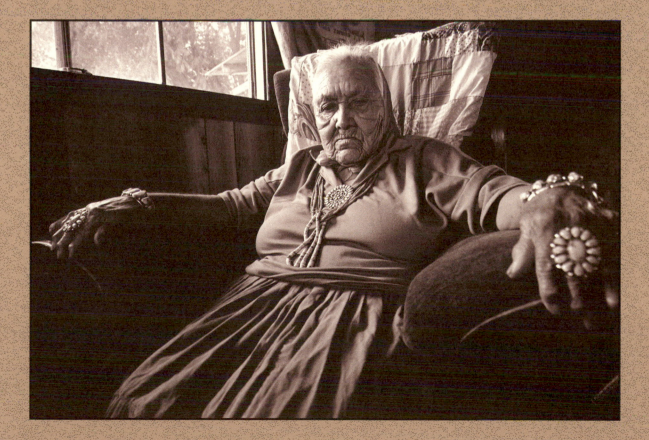

SPEAKING FOR COURAGE

Simon Ortiz

When I was a young man, maybe nineteen or twenty, and a college freshman in Colorado, I went to a conference for Southwest Indian youths at a university in Utah. I had pretty much decided by this time that I wasn't going to be a chemist after all. I wanted to be a writer— whatever that meant and however one went about becoming one.

I was being drawn, simply, toward what I always loved: stories and literature, and the act of writing that expressed them. I had grown up at Acoma Pueblo surrounded by stories and storytelling. It seemed that stories, especially the stories that came out of the oral tradition, offered explanations of just about everything. They held the narrative power of the mythic, a power that calls all things into existence and assures respect for life all around.

I had thought about a career as a writer in some fashion or other for quite a while. Years before, I had begun keeping a journal of sorts, and I tried my hand at poetry and songs. By the time I left high school, I was writing prose pieces that I claimed as "stories." Although haphazard in my creativity, I had a dedication that made me something of an "odd duck." Close friends often found themselves at the listening or reading end of my latest story or poem. And fantasies visited my imagination when I read biographies of people like Hemingway, Fitzgerald, Gauguin, or the works of Beat poets like Ginsberg and Snyder.

So there I was at the conference. And at a lunch of hamburgers and soda, a young Indian leader asked me what I wanted to be. "A writer," I said, rather impulsively. He looked at me with some puzzlement, then concern. "Don't even try," he warned. "You'll have a very difficult time of it." I was astonished and hurt. I respected this young Indian leader, and I expected him to be encouraging. It was the early 1960s, a new era for the nation and the human spirit, and almost anything seemed possible. "Why shouldn't I try?" I asked. "There are important things to say as an Indian, and I want to write about them."

"It's exactly because you're an Indian that you shouldn't try," he said. "You won't be accepted. No one wants to hear from Indians." Our conversation ended, but my disappointment lingered.

That was thirty years ago, but I remember it vividly. It was pivotal in my decision to become a writer, because it gave me a reason to write. I felt I could use my stories and poems to help Indian people come into visible and meaningful existence within a nation that denied their lives and culture.

"It's exactly because you're an Indian that you shouldn't try,"
he said. "You won't be accepted.
No one wants to hear from Indians."

25

Our culture, our identity,

is conveyed by language,

by the oral tradition.

Strange as it sounds, I wasn't really sure that writing stories and poems was the best way to express myself as an Indian. I felt that expressing myself in the "Mericano" language—English—was a modern-day trait that worked against me as an Indian, against all of us as Indians. Like most Indians of that time, I didn't trust the Mericano language, because it had been used so often to hurt us. English was the language of the dominant culture, of government, of treaties, of Indian schools where children were taught that there was something wrong with being Indian. Although I couldn't articulate it then, I had begun to realize that only when we had gained a stronger sense of our Indian selves would we be able to use English to express ourselves for who we are.

By comparison, the language of my childhood, the ancestral language of the Acoma Pueblo people—Aaquumeh hano—is imbued with a sacred and mythic power that embraces everything of spiritual and human importance. Our culture, our identity, is conveyed by language, by the oral tradition. It carries the knowledge of creation and existence. It is the way we perceive and express the meaning of our lives, the way we know ourselves as a strong and enduring people. And for this reason, it is sacred.

When I started writing, I wasn't wholly aware of the oral tradition, although it was always present in my consciousness. It was just "there," the very center of my Indian cultural identity, especially when I felt social pressure *not* to be different, *not* to be Indian, *not* even to be an ethnic minority. My consciousness as a writer was also deeply influenced by a responsibility "to help the people." As Aaquumeh youngsters, we were constantly reminded to heed our elders, including the old ones who had lived before. We were encouraged to serve and respect them and to attend to their words, especially when they spoke of our heritage and past, so that we, in turn, could pass this knowledge on to the next generation. It was often said that we existed because our ancestors loved, cared,

and prepared for us. They loved themselves, their land, and their way of life; they lived responsibly so that life would regenerate and flourish. And we were expected to do the same.

During the social upheavals of the late 1960s, this all-important credo—to help the people—was more relevant than ever. The struggles of Indian people were coming to the forefront of the nation's attention, and a resurgence of Indian cultural expression was a significant part of the fight. We insisted on our rights to land, water, fishing, and hunting. We demanded freedom of religion and cultural expression. As artists, we felt a good, invigorating strength in claiming who we were, some of us for the first time. As writers, we were able to use the Mericano language with a stronger sense of our cultural selves.

It is the way we perceive and express the meaning of our lives, the way we know ourselves as a strong and enduring people. And for this reason, it is sacred.

Our struggle to secure Indian rights had nationwide implications. Indian people were demanding access to land and ways of life that had been denied them since the "conquest" of the Americas—a notion that politicians, bureaucrats, and corporate chiefs found very problematic. It was apparently all right to venerate Indians as the "vanishing Red Man," "brave warrior," or "beautiful Indian princess." These images existed only in the imagination of the American public. But it was clearly *not* all right when real Indian people with sophisticated lawyers demanded that the United States respect the rights that are guaranteed to Indian people by treaty.

Although victories for American Indians have been few in the twentieth century, there is an important precedent: the return of Blue Lake to Taos Pueblo. In 1906, Blue Lake was taken, literally stolen, from the Pueblo by the U.S. Forest Service. Because they loved and respected their homeland, regarding it as the source of Creation, the people of Taos Pueblo began a legal struggle to regain Blue Lake. With persistence, patience, and courage rooted deeply in cultural belief, the elders of the Pueblo testified repeatedly at congressional hearings. There was never any thought of giving up—that would be like throwing away the credo of helping the people—and finally in 1971, the federal government returned sacred Blue Lake and some adjacent lands to Taos Pueblo. Their determination was truly epic, and their resource was the oral tradition and its mythic power to confirm existence and continuance.

It has required courage and complete faith in the wisdom of tradition to sustain our people and the remaining lands we hold tenaciously. Nothing else. When I decided to become a writer thirty years ago, there were important things to say as an Indian. And today, there are still pressing issues that have to be addressed by Indians *because we are Indians*. Government and business are still making claims on

Indian lands and lives. At my own Acoma Pueblo, for instance, the sacred lava lands of the nearby El Malpais region have been put under the jurisdiction of the National Park Service despite the vehement protests of Acoma leaders.

What will carry Indian people forward is faith in our Indian selves and in our responsibility to help each other. The oral tradition was always at the core of Indian consciousness. It has sustained my creativity as a writer and my commitment to help the people. Without this consciousness, this sense of self, I would not exist. And I believe this is true for Indian people throughout the Americas.

It will take courage and determined effort to acquire fully the justice we demand and to secure the continuance our oral tradition speaks of. Indian lives are at stake; there is no question about that. And there is a growing social and political ferment—not only in the United States but elsewhere. Look at Canada, Brazil, Bolivia, Guatemala, Peru, Ecuador, El Salvador, Mexico, all areas formerly inhabited solely by indigenous people. Anyone with a sense of compassion and responsibility must realize the necessity of a more hopeful vision.

This is a vision which we all can share, but it will have to come through a willing acceptance of Indian culture, a faith in the way Indian people have lived with Mother Earth and the Creators since the Beginning. This vision is held in the traditions and philosophy of a people who believe in continuance for themselves and for all life. Although only a beginning, this willingness to learn from Indian people and to join their struggle on behalf of "helping the people" is a vision of a good tomorrow we all need. This is progress and benefit for all people and all beings in Creation and Existence.

Seeing, Knowing, Remembering

Linda Hogan

On the day my grandmother died, the black and shining wet frog with golden eyes leapt against the wall, hitting it with a force that broke its spine. The grief for my grandmother was still too large for weeping, so I held the frog in my palm and cried for it. With fascination, I had watched the amphibious development of the frog, rescued from science-worshipping people. It seemed to reflect my own human growing, the way an egg divides, the pushing out of legs, how my own gill slit in the womb before birth vanished back into my still-wet skin. Like the frog, my grandmother and I lived between the elements, born to two worlds, Indian and white. And that white world was one that had come down, for Indian people, like a wall we were thrown against, a wall that turned our lives inside out, a wall that broke the spine of our societies.

Recently, Suzan Shown Harjo, director of the Morning Star Foundation, said, "When white people came here they threw a blanket over our heads. We are just now beginning to lift the corner of that blanket and see ourselves again." We are rising from the murky waters of history, surfacing like the crawfish of our tradition who brought clay up from unformed waters and fashioned the Earth. And it is true, we are just beginning to see and know each other, our pasts, our people. Only now is it safe. And we find ourselves still on the interrupted journey that our ancestors began. And coming into the light of this vision, I am beginning to see my grandmother.

Come from the Mound Builders, the brilliant calculators of time who stretched their hands in reverence toward the new moon, granddaughter of tribal leader Winchester Colbert, she was born in 1883. My grandmother lived through times that were astonishing in their horror: the Wounded Knee Massacre, deliberate policies of starvation and wars of extermination, the banning of Indian religions. The continent-wide stories of the suffering that befell other tribes traveled into Oklahoma, where the unbelievable tragedies were whispered in the night, and everyone knew it was a dangerous thing to be Indian. She witnessed what some would call the end, surviving through treaty-breaking times, gunpowder times, and later, the whirling sands of the Depression in a deforested Oklahoma. It was a time when belief and hope were assassinated, when it was understood that the white people feared and hated what was Indian, what was, to them, any form of wilderness or darkness or ancient ways.

"When white people came here they threw a blanket over our heads. We are just now beginning to lift the corner of that blanket and see ourselves again."

There was a hole in the world through which life itself was escaping. It was dangerous at home; my grandfather's sisters were forced to marry white men who wanted their land. There was no safety within the family; my grandmother's own father was an ambitious and dangerous man, a thief of Indian lands, a killer. Terror lived inside the familiar, inside what should have been love.

Like all other Chickasaw girls, my grandmother, Lucy, was a student at Bloomfield Academy, an Indian girls' school started by missionaries

in Indian Territory with the purpose of Americanizing the girls. I found her graduation exercises in the *Chronicles of Oklahoma*. She played a piano solo at commencement. Her sister recited "The Lotus Eaters" by Tennyson. Rev. Burris, an Indian orator, delivered the invocation in Chickasaw.

The girls were educated as if they were white, but leaving there, they returned to the Indian world.

Living in rural poverty, without water, my grandmother became a quiet, tender woman. The double knot of America was tied about her and inescapable. Like most of the Chickasaw women, she became an active churchgoer, practicing the outward shape of Christianity while retaining the depth of Indian traditional religion, a reverence for all life. She lived outside the confines of the white world within an older order, holding the fragments of an Indian way closed within her hands. She was the face of survival, the face of history and spirit in a

She was the face of survival, the face of history and spirit in a place where even women were forced to take up arms to protect themselves.

place where even women were forced to take up arms to protect themselves. At death, she made a statement of resistance; her gravestone disavowed Oklahoma statehood, the white world. It reads: Born and died in Berwyn Indian Territory.

I remember her as the old Indian woman of the turtles, who spoke to them and they listened, who wore aprons and cleaned fish, who cooked platters of eggs to feed her many grandchildren. She was the woman with never-cut hair. She was the blue-eyed Indian who used lye and ash to turn corn into white, tender hominy, cooking *pashofa* in a black kettle. There is even a recipe for "Lucy's Lye Soap." She was the woman, forced into English, who used snuff and healed her children with herbs, home remedies, and the occasional help of a black Chickasaw freedwoman named Aunt Rachel, a root worker. My grandmother was the beautiful lover of land, people, and quiet Oklahoma nights full of remembered fear, wet heavy  air, fireflies, and the smell of pecan trees, the land with tarantulas and rattlesnakes, the numerous and silencing sounds of gunshots in the night.

Like the old redwood forests, when a mother tree falls, a young one springs from its death. I am one of the trees grown out of my grandmother's falling at a time when Indian dances were still outlawed, gatherings suspect. One of the bare survivors of this history, lighter-skinned, broken, I rose out of the forbidden ways, a frog waking beneath the mud, feeling the vibration of rain, smelling water, digging out.

Like the old redwood forests,

when a mother tree falls,

a young one springs

from its death.

The line where my grandmother ends and I begin is no line at all. I am a child that once lived inside her, that was carried inside the builders of the mounds, the cells of mourners along the Trail of Tears. From them I still remember to honor life, mystery, and this incomparable ongoing creation.

And living at the secret heart of this creation, I am the grandmother now, traveling among those who cannot see or know me, learning the healing of plants, caring for children, struggling against the madness called progress, and believing the sun's old ways. I know this land is charged with life. I know what has happened to it, and to us. And I know our survival.

VOICES OF THE INVISIBLE

Debra CallingThunder

There are voices behind the wall—our voices, disembodied, spoken as if by beings unseen.

From the silence arise words conjured from invisible mouths, and laughter without smiles, and songs without celebration, and wailing without tears.

The air is crowded with words—wondrous and beautiful words that rise invisible and unheard and then are swallowed by time. The air is crowded with words—words that bind us to eternity, that carry the stories and dreams which are gifts from generations unseen, the songs of victory and mourning which compel us to seek tomorrow.

We are the invisible ones, the People of the Sky, the people of dreams whose voices cannot be bound by pain. We are the people of prayers, who stand small before the Creator, who entreat him, so that the strand of time that holds us to eternity might not be cut and our words slip into silence.

Words are gifts, our grandparents say, and they give us many words so that we will remain a nation, a circle of people.

∘∘∘

I give this song to Our People, to all the generations, and empty my
soul before them.

Words are gifts, our grandparents say, and they give us many words
so that we will remain a nation, a circle of people.

∘∘∘

My grandmother, Cleone Thunder, is nearly 90 now, an age she says
is not so old. Days disappear, falling furiously into time, but love
remains, and words and songs and stories.

She tells us the stories of our
beginning when the Creator
above rejoiced and we and
many others came to exist,
and the circle of our lodges
grew large. Only a short time
ago, she says, Our People
roamed the Earth, following
the great buffalo herds that
stormed across the plains,
across an expanse of time
and dreams.

The buffalo sang to us, and
their song was their life. The
buffalo sang to us so that we would grow strong. And the Old People
would gather together many words to make prayers to the Creator.
They would gather words as they walked a sacred path across the
Earth, leaving nothing behind but prayers and offerings.

Now the buffalo days are gone, and we are here, living on a reservation in houses, no longer in a circle of tipis, but still as a tribe. Many of us have fallen into material poverty, but we are rich in relatives and songs and beauty.

The transmission of these words is how we keep the oral tradition alive, the gift of the Old People who loved us from long ago even though we did not yet exist upon the Earth. The words of the grandparents have bound us together, those of us who are like a victory song, like an eagle feather, like the thunder when it laughs.

Many of us have fallen into material poverty, but we are rich in relatives and songs and beauty.

When my grandmother was young, she lived in the old way—in a tipi near the Wind River, the river we love—with her great-great-grandmother, Hoh-dah-wan, who gathered wood although she was old.

Hoh-dah-wan, the grandmother of Chief Black Coal, lived during a time when the people wandered the Earth, starving because the buffalo were nearly gone. She gave my grandmother the stories of the Sand Creek Massacre of 1864, when the U.S. Cavalry attacked a Cheyenne and Arapaho camp under a white flag of truce and an American flag.

On that November morning in what is now Colorado, our traditional homeland, Hoh-dah-wan saw old people, women, and children hunted down by soldiers. She saw the rape and mutilation of women, whom Our People considered sacred. She saw soldiers cutting open the bellies of pregnant women and fashioning toys from the breasts and female organs of dead women. The soldiers were ordered to seek out and kill young girls because "they breed like lice."

She saw the people fleeing in the snow, running to the riverbanks, hoping the Earth would shelter them from the nightmare.

After it was done, the soldiers looted the camp, stealing sacred objects and human bodies—including those of my grandmother's two uncles. The elders say that the loss of sacred objects continues to hurt the tribe.

The U.S. Army used the beheaded bodies for medical research. It later gave some of the remains to the Smithsonian Institution in Washington, D.C.—our national museum—for display as curios.

In October 1992, a Smithsonian anthropologist came to talk to the spiritual elders of our tribe about the repatriation of Arapaho human remains and funerary and sacred objects. My grandmother and I were there.

The Smithsonian has made the return of massacre victims' remains a priority, he told us that day nearly 128 years after the massacre. He said that the government began taking the remains of tribal people to continue medical studies begun on the bodies of Civil War soldiers.

No, my grandmother told him, it was because white people considered us savage and uncivilized. But they were wrong.

My grandmother is among the first Arapahos to know only the confines of a reservation and not to learn the sacred ways of the women's Quill Society.

Her mother, Grass Woman, the daughter of Black Coal, was one of the last of the seven medicine women who carried the Quill Society's medicine bundles. Until her time, the women had passed on knowledge of the society to successive generations.

The seven medicine women supervised the making of quill ornaments used to decorate tipis, moccasins, buffalo robes, and cradles with designs representing prayers for health and long life. The women made gifts of the quillwork so that blessings would follow the people as they traveled the four hills of life.

The ceremonies of the society have disappeared with other aspects of Arapaho life, and our grandparents say they long for the old ways. There is a loneliness for Arapaho words, they say—the quiet, flowing words of the storytellers that spilled into the thin, winter light and into the hearts of the people, the words that bound generations and were stronger than death.

The women made gifts of the quillwork so that blessings would follow the people as they traveled the four hills of life.

In 1878, the Northern Band of Our People settled on a reservation in Wyoming that they share with an enemy tribe, the Shoshone. The federal government set about turning them into farmers and Christians by allotting families land and outlawing the tribe's ceremonies. Smallpox threatened the tribe, which numbered only several hundred.

Black Coal, one of our last traditional chiefs, gave part of his land allotment to the Catholic Church for a school. That way, he said, the

children would no longer be sent to faraway boarding schools, banished from the words of Our People.

His son, Summer Black Coal, had been one of the first Arapahos to be taken to boarding school, where the children were punished for speaking their tribal languages. The sons of the Arapaho chiefs and subchiefs were taken so that the people would no longer fight and the future leaders would not learn Our People's way.

After the school at St. Stephen's Mission was built, the elders, the chiefs, and the warriors would go into the classrooms and tell the children to get a white man's education. The buffalo days are gone, they told them, and you are the ones who will make a new life for the people.

In 1958, the federal government and the state of Wyoming put a radioactive-waste dump near the school. It wasn't cleaned up until 30 years later.

The children were not sacred to them.

○○◎

In 1890, Smithsonian ethnologist James Mooney described Our People as "devotees and prophets, continuously seeing signs and wonders."

The government had sent him to study our tribe, because it expected us to become extinct and our words to fall into silence. It was during this time that many of the sacred societies, including the Quill Society, began to die out, and soon their ceremonies slipped away and their prayers were heard no more upon the Earth. It was also during this time that Our People began to follow the way of the Ghost Dance, crying out to the Creator, for the return of the buffalo and a way of life.

Have pity on us, Father, they prayed. Have pity on us, for we have nothing left.

The government had sent him to study our tribe, because it expected us to become extinct and our words to fall into silence.

We buried my cousin last month. He was seventeen.

Before we buried him, the priest said words, incantations. He told us that all of us were to blame for his death because we failed to speak, we failed to listen. He said that we loved alcohol too much and our young ones too little.

His words cut into the silence and into our hearts.

Then, we heard the songs given to us by the Old People, the healing words that rose above the circle of the drum. They sang so that we would be strong and the people endure. We have done it many times before—given our young ones back to the Earth who catches our tears and to the Creator above.

We have done it many times before, we, the Sky People who are tied together by time and blood, who have shared laughter and tears, life and death.

In July 1992, my family visited the Plains Indian Museum in Cody,

Wyoming, where traditional cradleboards were on display, including

an Arapaho cradleboard made around 1890 from sackcloth and dyed

porcupine quills.

A little girl asked her mother what the quill ornaments were.

Toys, her mother said.

She did not know that they were the captive prayers the grandmothers

had prepared for the young ones.

She did not know that like the sacred prayers of the grandmothers and

the songs of the buffalo, too many of our children have fallen silent.

FRIENDS, WE ARE ALL INDIANS

Mark Trahant

When I was about seventeen, my dad found an old box in our attic. Inside the box were stacks of a Shoshone-Bannock newspaper from the 1930s. *Tevope*, which means "paper" in the Shoshone language, was a crude typewritten monthly report reproduced by stencil.

As I flipped through the yellowing pages, I found words that seemed to be written for me.

"Friends, we are all Indians no matter how white or dark you are. It does not make any difference where you are, what you are doing, or how much money you are making. We are all Indians," wrote the editor Ralph Dixey in June of 1939.

"Our chiefs call us half-breeds and no good and we call them darn fools. Now, who is right? We are both wrong. We are all Indians."

These words spoke to me, because I had trouble figuring out who I was. I am a mixed-blood. My father's side of the family is Shoshone-Bannock, Assiniboine, and French. My mother is a mixture of Scottish and other European nationalities.

When I lived in California with my mother, I was called an Indian. When I lived with my father on the Fort Hall Indian Reservation, I was considered what Shoshones call a *neme tybo*, which means part human and part white.

Who is an Indian? The whole notion of "Indianness" can be troubling. To be sure, there is the issue of race—"blood quantum" as it is coldly called by the federal government. But there are also issues of citizenship and culture. Although I was an enrolled member of the Shoshone-Bannock tribe, I faced difficult questions about my cultural identity, about just how Indian or white I considered myself to be. How was I—a gangly high-school kid— supposed to know the answer to a question that has vexed Indian people, tribes, and federal policymakers for more than two centuries?

Fifteen years later, I began to realize that identity is a complicated question for my generation. Whether we like it or not, the youth of Indian country are bombarded by cultural influences—from television to telephones—that are bound to change tribal cultures. And that change is important to me for two reasons. First, because it isn't new. All cultures change. It's a part of life and part of survival. The second reason is that it affirms that it's OK to be a mixed-blood. It's who I am. I can take up the best traits of both sides of my family and make up the person that is me.

This notion of change runs contrary to the mythic image of the American Indian. For some people the only "real Indian" is a "traditional Indian"—clad in buffalo robes, adorned with feathers, astride a horse—the classic Hollywood stereotype. This buckskin image of the Plains Indian is indeed a part of my history, but so too are suit-wearing tribal leaders. So-called Indian aficionados don't seem too happy about the suit-wearing type. They're often disappointed to learn that Indians wear regular clothes and that sometimes they dress more like cowboys than Indians. Nor are they too pleased when they learn that the majority of Indian people identify themselves as Christians (at least nominally), although this certainly doesn't preclude participation in Native religions.

Fact is, Indian people live in a multiethnic, multiracial world just like everyone else in this country. They've always made alliances, intermarried, and borrowed ideas and technology from other people. This can be a productive process, a source of great vitality and innovation. Indian history didn't end in the 1800s. Indian cultures aren't some sort of museum piece that are frozen in time, preserved under glass. They evolve, grow, and continually try to renew themselves.

For example, take the Navajos, one of the country's largest tribes. Located in the cultural crossroads of the American Southwest, the Navajos have always been willing to learn from other people in order to revitalize their own culture. They are adept cultural borrowers, taking useful tools and practices from their Indian, Hispanic, and Anglo neighbors— things like horses, pottery, and silver—and transforming them into something distinctly Navajo. They adopted other Indians, establishing new clans. Even Spaniards joined the Navajos, becoming the Nakai or Mexican clan.

I recently married a Navajo woman. On the day of our wedding, the question I asked myself as a seventeen-year-old youth came back to me. Before the ceremony, the medicine man asked, "Are you an Indian?" He was asking me who I was and if I believed in the way of the ceremony.

"Yes," I said. "I am Shoshone-Bannock."

"Good," he said, "the ceremony will mean more because you know who you are."

We were married in a traditional Navajo ceremony. My family entered the hogan first, bearing gifts for my wife's family and a saddle: a sign that I was ready to make a new home. Then my wife's family entered the hogan carrying corn mush prepared by her grandmother. White cornmeal, representing the woman's family, was mixed with the male's yellow cornmeal and set in a wedding basket. My wife and I grabbed fingerfuls of mush and ate them, and we were married. Two lives combined into one. Navajos say it is a new life.

This simple ritual reaffirmed my belief that the future of Indian culture rests on our ability to sort out which traditions we must keep alive and which ones we must adapt. As a gangly teenager, I had no say in my race, but when I married I declared my identity and my future. I am a citizen of the Shoshone-Bannock tribe, but I am also part white and, so important now, a *shadanii*, a Navajo in-law.

A new life? Yes, there is that too. Our son, Marvin Sam, named after his grandfathers, was born last year. And now, as a father, I want him to know that life is about change, that he can move in many worlds and learn from many traditions, and that we must keep fighting to make things better for our relations. My son is a citizen of the Navajo Nation, but I hope he will draw freely on Shoshone-Bannock, Assiniboine, European, and American traditions to create his better world.

GOING HOME, DECEMBER 1992

Paula Gunn Allen

And thus, beneath a clear,

cold January sky,

emboldened by righteous

rage and plentiful hope,

I set out to seek the

American grail in the

promised Golden State.

I left New Mexico, my home, almost twelve years ago. I was depressed because the state had voted for Ronald Reagan. My mother called me on election night to crow: "We're so happy!" Her voice betrayed a hint of gloat beneath its familiar warmth. At that time, fury, or simmering rage at any rate, was how I moved from one life stage to another, though it had been a capricious master. It had motivated my writing, my curiosity, and my intellectual pursuits, and it had colored my career and my relationships, often disastrously, for a number of years. That year, just after Ronald Reagan's election, rage moved me to California. On that cold election night, I made my plans to escape the confinements of rage, disappointment, rejection, and fear. On Martin Luther King Jr.'s birthday, I headed west along the familiar highway to the Bay area, a song by the Police ringing in my head: "So if you're dreaming about California...."

A small trailer hitched behind my car held some household stuff, my typing table and chair, the three or four cartons of books that remained from thefts and giveaways, sales, and trashing. With me in the car—named White Spirit by the dealer—rode my crystal ball, Mitse; my IBM electric typewriter, unnamed; my lover, M.; and my precious backpack stuffed with poetry and fiction manuscripts, all named though unpublished. And thus, beneath a clear, cold January sky, emboldened by righteous rage and plentiful hope, I set out to seek the American grail in the promised Golden State.

Because my life had changed dramatically in the five years since I had last lived in the Bay area, I wasn't certain what I'd find there, other than a familiar city where gays clustered, where voting Democrat was thought to be somewhat reactionary, where fringe politics and alternative spiritualities thrived. I believed I was heading to California where the Aquarian Conspiracy was alive and well. It was January 1981, and although I didn't know it, California was indeed a brand new game.

Now it's December 1992. A little over a year ago we buried my mother. For the first time in years I returned to our homelands around Laguna. The day before her funeral, my children and I drove out to Laguna and Cubero, her first and longest home and the place where I grew up. The land was the strongest link between us. We climbed the mesa behind my grandma's house in Cubero, a climb made difficult by someone's addition of a fence just where the sandstone rears up behind my grandmother's rock garden. We performed a small ceremo-

ny of remembrance for my mother, burning and then burying the sage used the night before to soothe our grief. Nothing soothes it, really. The hard part is not being able to call her on the phone. In the time I've been gone, a score of family members and several friends have died, and I am not only sorrowing but old. It's strange to be the old folks when you're not really out of childhood, however gray your hair under the wishful red dye.

I had not returned to Laguna or Cubero since my grandmother died seven years before. It was too painful to go where Grandma's chirpy voice no longer greets me with news of scattered family, where there is no cup of her strong black coffee, no Pepperidge Farm cookies stashed carefully against occasions, no little lunch. Too painful to go where there is no tiny Grandma standing at the kitchen door, guiding me with her eyes and voice as I enter her rock garden, disappear behind the pussy willow bush she nurtured for thirty years, and climb toward the ancient sandstone cliffs that were so much my childhood home.

It was only when Mother died that I returned to Laguna, hoping to find her spirit on the mesas above her home, hoping to meet her on an odd volcanic rock we called "the Chair," spewn from an explosion thousands of years ago, landing miles away from the eruption. It was about the size of a Barcalounge, high-backed with an inward-curving seat. It stood sentinel near the highest point of the mesa, and I had spent hours there all through my growing up. I visited it every time I went home. I went to the Chair on the mesa during marriages and love affairs, through breakups, pregnant, with children, alone. I took my best friend there. I took three husbands and two lovers.

So at Mother's death I returned, an aging and grieving woman. Mother wasn't there, only the wind, mysterious in its soughing; only faded memories, great, gaunt vistas, November light, and cold, cold wind. You can see the entire little village from the Chair; you can see eons of Earth's life; you can see millennia of all that is past and returns no more. My mother climbed those mesas in her youth, like her daughter, like her daughter's daughter, like our sons. They were much different mesas then, overlooking a different world.

What I realized on that mesa on that bleak day before my mother's funeral was only that I had not known the woman at all—so private she was, so inward-bound. Who were you, I asked the wind? The silence that holds it in the air was the answer I received: I am myself, and no other.

Mother used to tell me that I might have to go along with whatever was required. I might have to say a lot of things I didn't mean, didn't believe. But, she would say, touching her brow with an extended finger, they can't control what you think: that's for you alone. A few

So at Mother's death I returned, an aging and grieving woman. Mother wasn't there, only the wind, mysterious in its soughing; only faded memories, great, gaunt vistas, November light, and cold, cold wind.

years ago we talked about that privacy. She repeated her lesson, adding: there's a line all the Indian people have that no one can cross. Behind that line I keep everything that is mine, that is me. I don't let anyone over that line. Maybe we're different that way, she said, pausing. Maybe that's what makes us what we are. It's not the same as "keeping secrets," no. It is simply recognizing that one's self is inviolate; the private soul is private, not public. It's neither commodity nor

consumable. It is most like the center of silence that is the always-flowing wellspring of life, like the spring that used to bubble up like a miracle just beyond the alfalfa field which was across the little arroyo from our old house in Cubero—the sweet, sweet spring where every day my mother went to draw water for her family's use.

+++

Now, on this gloom-filled late December day nearly a year since Mother's death and twelve years since I moved to California, I'm heading back down the highway, going home. My stuff has grown by leaps and bounds. Laden with possessions and bills, possessed of three grandchildren all lost to the red mists of their three separate mothers' rage, sans lover, sans mother, deserted by both rage and hope, I make my painful journey home, a wounded eagle returning to the ancient nest. Pursued by tornado warnings, brain-fogged after a night of hurricane-like storms that beat around my daughter's Marin County home until dawn, I turn eastward on Highway 58 toward Bakersfield, toward home, toward Laguna and Cubero. I anticipate driving by the villages just after the new year begins. Speeding by them on I-40, I will remember scores of stories from my life there, the people I knew, very old, lost, dead. I don't think I'll stop. I will speed around them, along the edges. The way of respect, the way of non-violation. My mother's and grandmother's way, the Laguna way. There is still a *there*, there but not one I recall.

I left home premenopausal, debilitated from not-yet-diagnosed Chronic Fatigue Immune Deficiency Syndrome; now postmenopausal, in better health after acupuncture, Chinese herbs, good chiropractic care, and a California-decreed upscale diet. Then, I was an angry daughter determined to flee the redneck politics of my home, my parents, and my bewildered childhood. I return a grieving daughter, a grieving granddaughter, a grieving grandmother, a single, aging woman whose own daughter rages somewhere in the California fantasy I'm leaving behind. My typewriter has transformed into a powerbook, a portable printer, and a PC. My crystal ball is goddess-knows-where, replaced by eagle feathers, my great-grandmother's huge Acoma pot, and a beautiful basket that I think is Pima—or is it Apache?—also once hers. Broke again (or is it still?), I gotta sell them both, soon.

I will miss them, as I will miss the seductive heaps of fresh vegetables and fruit that grace California markets and street stands. I will miss the softly feminine California hills, the redwoods, the fog, the benefi-cent climate. I have lost much in these twelve years. The edge of the gathering storm I've so far outpaced is a fitting mentor for this newer, older phase. Mournful, sodden, the shaman sky mumbles companion-ably all around as I drive south, then east: going always brings return.

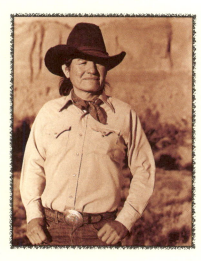

On Christmas afternoon, just a few days before I left California, a package of photographs was delivered to me at my daughter's home—the photographs that are in this book. I reached for one stack eagerly, because the photograph of a man holding a silver-tipped cane strongly reminded me of my uncle Ook, who died five or six years ago. Intrigued, I pulled it out of its covering and stared at it for a time, remembering Ook, smiling, torn. The last time I saw him was in a dream. He was happy enough, once again driving the old milk truck for Creamland Dairies as he had twenty or thirty years before. I guess he wanted me to know he was OK, or to see how I was doing. And I remembered him, a much younger man, dropping by to visit, tilting his chair at the oilcloth-covered table until my mother would say, "It's not a rocking chair! You're going to break it! You're going to fall!" And the time he did fall—*whump!*—flat on his back. And the look on his face, the laughter. "Well grace, did you enjoy your trip?" When he was ready to go on his way he'd amble toward the door, saying his customary "See you in the funny papers." I turned the photo over and saw it had been taken by a Laguna photographer, Lee Marmon, who is my cousin and Ook's, and who took the photos for my first wedding back in the 1950s. Of course the face looked familiar, though at the time I didn't recognize Walter Sarracino, past governor of Laguna Pueblo and also a relative, holding one of the governor's canes presented to the Pueblos by Abraham Lincoln.

I called my youngest son to look. Quietly we went through the stacks together, murmuring. Among hundreds of images were a precious few photos of home. They were, except for my children's presence, the best gift I received, even though I knew that most of the pictures, maybe all of them, had been taken years before and probably chronicled people dead, disappeared, or grown much older than their frozen images from another time. I realize as I drive beneath the lowering clouds that these wonderful photos, static and dead, preserve a subtle lie. Life in its unfolding does not stop, even though life and love both have their finite terms.

I am going home. I left in anger and return in grief. The road that unwinds before me cannot be the same one I took all those years ago. Even the mountains, soaring and serene, the great plains spreading below, the laddered mesas that climb the horizon to meet the rain-blest clouds will not be the ones I left behind. There is a new life brewing beneath the rain-bearing clouds, and I shall drive through the storm all the way to old heart's place, brand-new home.

LARRY MCNEIL

© Larry McNeil

By Our Hand, Through the Memory, the House Is More Than Form

Elizabeth Woody

In contemplating the house of my childhood, the one that I grew up in, it is not the structure or the condition of the house I recall as much as the sentiments about dwelling and homeland that gave strength to its structure.

My childhood home was fourteen miles from the Warm Springs Reservation, in the town of Madras, Oregon. We were some 160 miles removed from the Columbia River and the pathways of the salmon that my mother's people cherished, celebrated, harvested, dried, and incorporated into their lifeways for over 14,000 years. Few will understand how we came to be so far removed from our ancestral homeland of the Columbia River system, which carries large volumes of water inexorably to the Pacific Ocean. The geography of our landscape—the snowcapped Cascade range of volcanoes, surrounded by evergreen forests and high desert—is an integral element of the culture of the Plateau, as we are collectively called. I belong to a people who cherished the land.

My maternal grandparents were the first of several generations to be born within the reservation boundaries after the treaty of 1855 at Walla Walla, Washington, between "the Bostons" (as U.S. citizens were called by the Plateau people) and the political affiliations of people present-ly called "tribes." We had not called our people "tribes" prior to the treaty, as it is a term brought from feudal Europe. It is better to think of the basic component of Plateau society as having been set up for participants of shared political principles, living in  villages governed by a leader who was not subject to outside authori-ties. Decisions were made by acclamation, and those who disagreed moved to another village.

The nature of our current regard for and belief in these inhabitants of the past is more than participation in the old coexistent economic sys-tem of task sharing and consensus. It is more than the ethno-racial identity of the citizens. It is the pre-existent honoring and knowledge of the land that held the people together. Human beings flourish with a conscious regard for all beings, for the place that holds their lives, for the deceased, and for their stories of creation and creating. To speak of the spiritual in this context is too personal to present arbi-trarily. That sense is a common bond we have with our bodies and share with one another, which I feel requires no explanation.

In the house of my childhood, my grandfather, Lewis Pitt Sr., was a Wasco/Wishram/Watlala (Cascade/English) descendant of the ancient Fisher people, who made distinctive art objects of X-ray figures, male

and female, of people, ancient sturgeon, condor, and deer. He spoke six dialects of Sahaptin and Chinookan Northwest indigenous languages as well as the intertribal trade language—Chinook Jargon. My grandmother, Elizabeth Thompson Pitt, a descendant of the Wyampum and a smaller Deschutes River band, was born and raised at the Hot Springs now known as Kah-nee-ta Resort. She was as settled on this land as the old junipers, the volcanic formations, and hillsides that she loved to walk about on. She was an artisan and possibly, for a time, a healer. She made sure that we understood her reverence for the land and the traditional beliefs by taking us as children to the places where the people gathered for worship—places filled with symbolism and ceremony.

He was an "Agency" man, she a "Simnasho" woman. Two small gatherings of longhouses and houses, churches and tule shacks, and families—two distinctive cultural communities on the reservation. When they married, each planted a cedar tree, side by side. The trees intermingled their roots and boughs, symbolizing the tentative touchings of two separate beings. In the structures where these people gathered we heard all the many different languages spoken by both my grandparents and all the neighbors and visitors, but in their children they encouraged the use of English. They brought into it a passion for expression, and in that passion, a love for all things.

They moved off the reservation to be nearer to the schools for their three children. In this move, my grandmother was distanced from her immediate connections to her relatives and from the beading circles, healing gatherings, celebrations, winter dances, and the casual visiting at the general store/post office. She had to adjust to her new location.

We were some 160 miles removed from the Columbia River and the pathways of the salmon that my mother's people cherished, celebrated, harvested, dried, and incorporated into their lifeways for over 14,000 years.

85

My uncle, Lewis Jr., recalls that she took refuge in her bedroom. Her room held the many bundles of the beaded objects, cornhusk bags, and Klickitat baskets inherited from our relatives. It seemed that to visit these things was to contact the thoughts of relatives who had passed on. The house brightened when she decided to make some leggings. For the first time alone, she drew her pattern and started

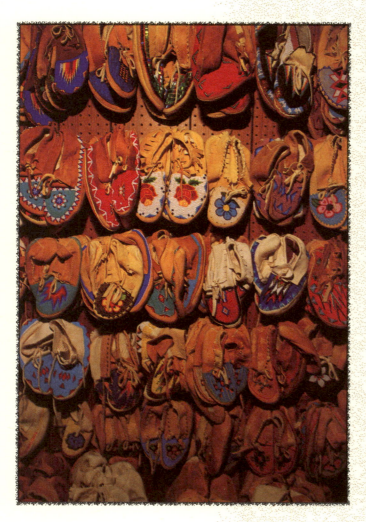

beading. She asked Lewis Jr., "Do you like my leggings?" He was ecstatic, "Yes, they are beautiful." He knew at that moment, by the startling burst of her creativity, in her pleasant circle of light, that they would be all right in their new home.

It is this blessing of being able to make things that reconstructs my life, that gives me the knowledge to restore myself. The things I saw—the collaborative living structures, the places of worship and feasts, the outfits of antiquity, the buckskin garments, the beaded objects, the woven baskets for subsistence, the cradleboards for protection, the feathers of prayer, the couriers to a higher thought—are still magnificent. They were made, traded, and collected by great-grandparents and by living relatives, and I saw that they loved deeply.

These messages—the beaded birds, horses, trees, stars, and geometric abstractions—are like prayer, a prayer for our present world to know again the root connection to our existence. The Earth provided for us, and through the Earth we prosper and absorb into ourselves the potency of life.*

* All these objects were made from the Earth and did not disrupt its systems. The events and stories elaborated the cultural significance of place through the coupling of land and experience. The perspective and treatment of land, animals, and things to events during our tenure and to myth told in current life made the experience of telling and retelling a source of inspiration.

To be a granddaughter was my privilege; to be a daughter, a niece, a sister, a cousin an honor. In this honor, this state of being respected, I thrived. To thrive is to learn how to respect others and how to act with courage, humility, generosity, and compassion. Although this is simple to say in English and is overused in daily language, it is complex to be an independent being, responsible to the nuances and dynamics of ancestral continuity.

As a segment of the great weaving of cultures, which is continuous and as ancient as the mastodon and condor who have perished from this area, it is only ingenuity and the simple intention to live well that rendered the ability to endure. Our legacy is that we still live, in some manner, in congruence with the past, not in a linear fashion, as people tend to think of time, but cyclically, in accordance with the cycles that are as efficient as the spirals found in baskets and shells and petroglyphs.

After speaking about artistic collaboration at a recent conference, a Wasco "aunty" told me, "Collaboration, in our language, is also the word for science." I feel that this includes nature, which holds everything and which directs the patterned chaos and the tranquillity of being complete, even in its smallest form. Our language, now physically unspoken in my life but active in my brain, has a lucid regard for our environment.

To thrive is to learn how to respect others and how to act with courage, humility, generosity, and compassion.

Like them, we repair our culture and make it anew. The secret vitality of our imaginations presents itself all around us as this Earth, Homeland, and House of Livelihood and Rest. All around this story, the eyes look into the sway of our industrious behavior, the hands move back to the beginning each time we work with material from the land. We listen, absorbed in the story by blood, by association, listening with the part that is internally one self and many selves. In the sound of water, the sheen of river stone, a song is pervasive and faithful to continuance, and the memory in its own language tells the story well.

VISION, IDENTITY, AND THE GREAT MYSTERY

White Deer of Autumn (Gabriel Horn)

Who are we? Where are we going? Why are we here? Imagine if more people searched the Mystery of their lives for the answers to these questions. Imagine if more people understood the passion of the Lakota war cry: "It's a good day to die!" or the feelings of a man like Henry David Thoreau when he said that he would hate to face his death knowing that he had not lived. Imagine if the hearts of more people became like theirs…and the land became mother…and that which they share all things with became the Great Holy Mystery. Imagine….

The small stone was about the size of a marble. It had been painted

with a sacred red ochre by an Arapaho medicine man. Only he and

one other Arapaho man knew where this sacred paint could be found.

I was a young man alone on my first vision quest.

It was dawn. A strong salty breeze swept across the turquoise sea. It caused Gulf waters to ripple and the waves to swell and break into cool white crystals of foam that carried in the tide. I sat on the shore on my turquoise mat within a circle I had drawn in the bone-white sand. Golden sea oats and tall sea grass swayed near me.

They cast shadows around a round stone I had placed on the ground. The small stone was about the size of a marble. It had been painted with a sacred red ochre by an Arapaho medicine man. Only he and one other Arapaho man knew where this sacred paint could be found. I knew only that it was a journey which took him deep into the Wind River Mountains of Wyoming.

I can remember the night he returned with the paint and held the small stone with the fingers of one hand while he placed the fingers of his other into a small deerskin pouch, how he moved them around inside until they emerged glistening in dark crimson, how he rolled the small round stone between his fingers, mixing it with the paint until the stone turned red too.

A few days before my first vision quest I had fallen into my old uncle's arms and cried, for I'd just been fired from my first teaching position at an Indian high school. My marriage was falling apart. I had lost any sense of purpose and direction. These things conspired to make the long trip from Wyoming to my home in Florida even longer. Crossing such a distance seemed only to give my emotions more time to well up inside of me, so when I finally arrived at Uncle Nip's, I was a storm ready to release itself. And I did. It was as if all I had worked for in college and whatever semblance of identity I had struggled for was suddenly torn asunder. I was a broken man whose ideals were as scattered as a flock of frightened gulls. I seemed lost and afraid. I felt alone. And I cried in my old uncle's arms.

"Go for a vision," Nippawanock said, his wrinkled hands on my shoulders, his starry eyes penetrating my darkness. "It's time. If you are to walk the path of heart, then it is time...."

"Take your red stone with you to a place where you can be close to nature...a place where people won't disturb you. Use your medicine stone as your intercessor. Speak through it to the Mystery. Go from sunrise as long as you can but no more than four days. Don't eat, and don't drink. Concentrate on that part of you that is all things. Concentrate on the Mystery. Meditate."

I did what Uncle Nip advised and headed for the Island-Where-The-Great-Turtles-Nest. For days and nights I sat on my turquoise mat within the circle I had drawn in the sand as I called out into the Mystery for some understanding to my life. I wept for all the things I'd lost and for all those I had loved. Sometimes I shivered in terror at night, at having to face my own fears. Sometimes I lay silent, staring up at the stars. I remember how the sun rose each morning regardless of my state of mind and how the sudden emergence of dolphins made me feel light-headed and happy. I remember how the sun rose hot and lingered long and lasting...how it burned as I faced my own anger.

And although I received great insight that time years ago when I was a young man seeking a vision, no vision came to me. "The vision will come when you are ready," said Uncle Nip. "It will come at that special moment when time transcends reality and the Mystery of life reveals itself to you."

Unexpectedly, that would happen a year or so later on a cold wintry night in Minnesota. I had been teaching Indian children all day in the housing projects where the American Indian Movement school, Heart of the Earth, was located. And at night I had taught Indian adults in the basement of the Minneapolis Public Library. I had done this for days at a time, and living alone, I had no one to insist that I take time enough to eat or even to sleep.

I can remember the circle of elms and the snowy, sloping hills across the street from Powderhorn Park, where I lived. I can still recall standing outside under one of the great elms and gazing up at the glistening stars...how many more there seemed to be that night...how some of them seemed so big and close I could touch them if I reached out my hand.

Instead, the stars reached out to me, and a Being robed in red appeared before me. His eyes were large and shaped like almonds and as black as the stone of Apache tears. He motioned for me to look, and I saw the spirit-breath of my people fading. Then he motioned

again, and I saw a woman as old as the Earth. She spoke about lies and half-truths, about ambiguities and manipulations of words. When I turned away, the Being robed in red held in his hands a book of stars. He pointed to a certain place among them, and then the book of stars became the pipe that I would one day keep and protect with my life.

The vision I was given that night under the stars at Powderhorn, a thousand miles from the island where I first cried for one, became the guiding force and anchor of my life. Whenever I need to know whether or not I am doing the right thing for the People and the land, I recall my vision. If whatever I contemplate on doing is connected to that moment of Vision, then I know it's the right thing to do. And though time and experience and living in the Wheel has provided me dreams and ceremony, nothing has ever been like the Vision. It has kept me on the path of heart. It is the one thing that I know can never be taken away from me.

As I travel through the autumn of my life, I find myself wondering about things more than I used to. I wonder how we can ever have a planet where people live in peace if people don't seek out their place in the Mystery. I wonder how we can ever have peace in this world if people no longer feel their connectedness, their oneness with all things living together in the Great Holy Mystery. I wonder if we live in a land that will someday be called A-Place-Without-Vision.

I try to understand how it must feel not to be connected to every-thing in some magical, mysterious way? What would it be like not to live within the Wheel? What would it be like not to feel that the Earth is our Mother? What would it be like not to recognize that all Earth's creatures are our relatives? Is that why such people can slaughter dolphins and whales and each other? Is that why they can destroy forests, poison rivers, and pollute oceans? Is that why they can dump toxic waste into the land—because they do not regard it as their mother? Is it like being fragmented and not whole? Is it an act of rage?

I wonder how we can ever have a planet where people live in peace if people don't seek out their place in the Mystery.

I recall a time when I was young that someone stood among the ferns outside our house and asked me how much Indian I was. He insisted that I couldn't be a full-blood because of the green tint to my brown eyes. He also told me that he had studied Indians a lot in college and

had learned that there were hardly any full-bloods left. For some reason, I told him I was half. My uncle had heard me. When I went inside, old Nip asked me which half of me was Indian and which half of me wasn't. I felt foolish. Then he told me to close my eyes and ask my heart what I was. My heart never hesitated. I was Indian.

That night Uncle Nip handed me a necklace, one I'd seen him working on for several days. Before he placed it around my neck, he told me that the turquoise was Persian and the beads were European.

He said that only the deer antlers were from America. A steel wire connected everything.

"Our people don't come in parts," Uncle Nip explained. "Either you are an Indian, or you are not." Then he placed the necklace around my neck. As I studied it, he said, "Dissimilar things were fitted together to make something beautiful and whole."

How many children who identify as Indians can withstand the daily challenges: How much Indian are you? Why is your skin so light? Why is it so dark? Why is your hair brown? Why is it curly? You can't be all Indian—your eyes are blue. What's your tribal number?

Then he placed the necklace around my neck. As I studied it, he said, "Dissimilar things were fitted together to make something beautiful and whole."

How many children can withstand such challenges to their identity without learning the importance of a vision? Without a vision, they may grow up allowing others to tell them who they are. They may even think that being an Indian is something defined by a government. But when they have a vision, they know who they are. They know how much Indian they are.

I can remember gazing up at the stars the night of my vision. I can remember feeling like I wanted to touch them. I felt so close to them...I felt a part of them. I remember watching dolphins the time I cried for a vision and how good they made me feel. I felt a part of them. I remember putting the ashes of my Uncle Nip into the Earth and thanking her for sustaining his life. And I felt a part of the land. "In some mysterious and wonderful way you are part of everything, Nephew. And in that same mysterious and wonderful way, everything is a part of you. That is the Great Holy Mystery. It always was and always will be."

It is with such an awareness that I've traveled in the Wheel. Twenty years after I first sought a vision, I sit again near my Florida home on the shore of the Gulf waters, and I wonder. The warm salty breeze blows across my mind, and the sunlight shimmering on the surface of the sea helps reality to transcend. And I can imagine!

THE KAW RIVER RUSHES WESTWARD

Luci Tapahonso

They had been dancing and singing for six days and nights already. From across the river valley, the songs drifted into our last waking moments, into our dreams.

North of our home in Lawrence, Kansas, the Kaw River flows wide and brown. When I first saw this river, I was surprised at how deep and how loud it is. Its banks are lined with thick groves of trees. In comparison, the San Juan and Rio Grande rivers in New Mexico are clear and shallow.

One fall we drove home to Shiprock, New Mexico—about 1,300 miles away. Our route took us across Kansas, into Colorado, and then down into northwestern New Mexico. It was such a contrast to see the wide fierce water of the Kaw and the quiet shallow San Juan in New Mexico. The terrain in Kansas is mostly rolling hills and flat plains, and as the rivers changed, the landscape did also, ranging from steep canyons and mountain gorges to the Rio Grande riverbed and then to the San Juan, which is a mile south of my parents' home. The night we arrived in Shiprock, I was very much aware that the river nearby was quiet, reflecting the dark sky and stars above. Alongside this river are huge old cottonwoods; willows and tamarack bushes are tucked along the sandy cliffs.

We drove into the yard late at night, and my parents were awake, waiting for us. After we ate a long-awaited meal of mutton stew and *náneeskaadí* (tortillas), we went to bed. It was dark and quiet in the house of my childhood. My daughter and I talked quietly a while before we fell asleep. In the dark-

ness, we heard the faint songs of the Yeis, the grandfathers of the holy people, and the low, even rhythm of the drum. They had been dancing and singing for six days and nights already. From across the river valley, the songs drifted into our last waking moments, into our dreams. While we slept, they sang, praying and giving thanks for the harvest, for our return and for the hundreds of others who returned home that weekend for the fall festivities. The Yeis danced for all of us—they danced in their fatigue, they danced in our tired dreams. They sang for us until their voices were hardly more than a whisper. Around three in the morning, they stopped to rest.

The next morning, we woke refreshed and happy. The morning air was clear and crisp with a harvest chill, and there across the blue valley stood Shiprock, a deep purple monolith. I drank coffee outside, watched the dogs act silly, and then I caught up on news of what had happened since my last trip. While we ate breakfast, my father watched news, the table radio played Navajo and English songs alternately, my mother told me a little story about when she was four or five years old,

I braided my daughter's hair, and two of my sisters came to visit. This is the familiar comfort I felt as a child, and it is the same for my children. The songs that the Yeibicheii sang, that the radio played, and that my mother hummed as she cooked are a part of our memories, of our names, and of our laughter. The stories I heard that weekend were not very different from the stories I heard as a child. They involved my family's memories, something that happened last week, and maybe news of high school friends. Sometimes they were told entirely in Navajo and other times in a mixture of Navajo and English.

There is such a love of stories among Navajo people that it seems each time a group gathers, the dialogue eventually evolves into sharing stories and memories, laughing, and teasing. To be included in this is a distinct way of showing affection and appreciation for each other. It is true that daily conversations strengthen us as do the old stories of our ancestors which have been told since the beginning of the Navajo time.

Just as the rivers we followed home evolved from the huge, wide Missouri River to the shallow water in the San Juan riverbed, the place of my birth is the source of my work and identity. My work ranges from stories I heard as a child, to stories that were told by relatives, friends, or colleagues, and to other poems and stories that are based on actual events. Most of my poems and stories originate in Navajo, either orally or in thought, and many have a song that accompanies the work.

The combination of song, prayer, and poetry is a natural form of expression for many Navajo people. A person who is able to "talk beautifully" is well thought of and considered wealthy. To know stories, remember stories, and to retell them well is to have been "raised right"; the family of such an individual is also held in high esteem. The value of the spoken word is not diminished, even with the influences of television, radio, and video. Indeed, it seems to have enriched the verbal dexterity of colloquial language, as for instance, in the names given to objects for which a Navajo

word does not exist, such as *béésh nitséskees* (thinking metal) for computers and *chidí bijéí* (the car's heart) for a car battery.

I feel fortunate to have access to two, sometimes three languages, to have been taught the "correct" ways to use these languages, and to have the support of my family and relatives. Like many Navajos, I was taught that the way one talks and conducts oneself is a direct reflection of the people who raised her or him. People are known, then, by their use of language.

It is with this perspective that I share my stories, poetry, and prayers. Once my oldest brother said about my *nálí*, my paternal grandmother, who died decades ago: "She was a walking storybook. She was full of wisdom." Like many other relatives, she had a profound understanding of the function of language. My words, then, are not "mine," but a collection of many voices that range from centuries ago and continue into the future.

For many people in my situation, residing away from my homeland, writing is the means for returning, for rejuvenation, and for restoring our spirits to the state of *hohzo* (beauty), which is the basis of Navajo philosophy. It is a small part of the "real thing," and it is utilitarian, but as Navajo culture changes, we adapt accordingly.

I view my writing as a gift from my mother and father, both of whom embody the essence of Navajo elders—patience, wisdom, humor, and courage. My writing is a collaboration of sorts with my sisters and brothers, my extended family, my friends, and especially my daughters and husband. Their thoughts, humor, and encouragement sustain me and all I undertake. *Ahéhee'*.

We are the invisible ones,

the People of the Sky,

the people of dreams whose voices

cannot be bound by pain.

We are the people of prayers,

who stand small before the Creator,

who entreat him, so that the strand

of time that holds us to eternity

might not be cut and our words

slip into silence.

—Debra CallingThunder

EDITOR

JOHN GATTUSO is editor of Stone Creek Publications in Philadelphia. His writing has appeared in publications including *The Washington Post*, *The Seattle Times*, and *New York Newsday* as well as a variety of travel books. He is the project editor and principal writer of *Insight Guide: Philadelphia* (1993) and *Insight Guide: Native America* (1992), a guide to American Indian communities and cultures in the United States. He is also editor of *Heart of the Earth: The Grand Canyon and Colorado Plateau*, a book of photographs and essays to be published by Stone Creek Publications in spring 1994. He lives in Philadelphia with his wife and two daughters.

WRITERS

PAULA GUNN ALLEN was born in Cubero, New Mexico, in 1939. She is of Laguna, Lakota, Scottish, and Lebanese descent. She is the author of several books of poetry, including *Skins and Bones*, *Wyrds*, *Star Child*, and *Shadow Country*; a novel, *The Woman Who Owned the Shadows*; and *The Sacred Hoop: Recovering the Feminine in American Indian Traditions*. She is the editor of *Studies in American Indian Literature* and *Spider Woman's Granddaughters*, an anthology of short stories which won an American Book Award from the Before Columbus Foundation in 1990. She was awarded the Native American Prize for Literature in 1990 for her entire body of work and the Vesta Literature Award in 1991. She was also named Woman of the Year in 1991 by the Southern California Women for Understanding. She is a professor of English at UCLA and is currently living in Albuquerque, New Mexico.

MICHAEL DORRIS, a member of the Modoc tribe, was born in 1945. Formerly a professor of anthropology and Native American studies at Dartmouth College, he now devotes his time to writing. He is the author of several works of nonfiction, including *The Broken Cord*, which was awarded the National Book Critics' Circle Award in 1989. His novels include *A Yellow Raft in Blue Water* and, most recently, *The Crown of Columbus*, co-authored with his wife Louise Erdrich, with whom he collaborates extensively. He is also the author of a children's book, *Morning Girl*, which won the Scott O'Dell Prize for Best Historical Fiction for Young Readers in 1992. His forthcoming books include a nonfiction work, *Rooms in the House of Stone*; a collection of essays, *Paper Trail*; and a collection of short stories, *Working Men*. Among his many awards and honors are a National Endowment for the Arts Fellowship in 1989 and an Indian Achievement Award in 1985.

JOY HARJO, an enrolled member of the Creek Nation, was born in Tulsa, Oklahoma, in 1951. She is a graduate of the Institute of American Indian Arts and the University of New Mexico, and she holds an MFA in creative writing from the Iowa Writers' Workshop. Her books of poetry include *What Moon Drove Me to This?*, *She Had Some Horses*, *In Mad Love and War*, and with photographer Stephen Strom, *Secrets from the Center of the World*. Her awards include the Josephine Miles Award for Excellence in Literature from PEN and the William Carlos Williams Award from the Poetry Society of America. Among works forthcoming are a children's book, a memoir, an anthology of Native women's writing, and a screenplay for the American Film Foundation. She is currently a professor of creative writing at the University of New Mexico in Albuquerque. In addition to writing, editing, and teaching, she plays saxophone with her band, Poetic Justice.

LINDA HOGAN, a member of the Chickasaw Nation, was born in Denver, Colorado, in 1947. Her published works include a novel, *Mean Spirit*; collections of poetry, *Eclipse*, *Seeing Through the Sun*, *Red Clay*, *Savings*, and her most recent work, *The Book of Medicines*. She is currently an associate professor of English at the University of Colorado, Boulder.

SIMON ORTIZ was born and raised in Acoma Pueblo, New Mexico. He has taught creative writing at California State University, San Diego; the University of New Mexico; and Sinte Gleska College on the Rosebud Reservation in South Dakota. Recent publications include *Fightin': New and Collected Stories*; a book of poetry, *From Sand Creek*, which received the Pushcart Prize for Poetry; and *Woven Stone*, his latest collection of poetry. He also edited *Earth Power Coming*, a collection of short fiction, and wrote the narrative of *Surviving Columbus*, a recent PBS documentary. He received the Native American Lifetime Achievement Award for Writing from the Returning the Gift Project in 1993. He lives in Santa Fe, New Mexico.

LESLIE MARMON SILKO was born in Albuquerque and grew up at Laguna Pueblo. She is the author of two novels, *Almanac of the Dead* and *Ceremony*; a collection of prose and poetry, *Storyteller*; and a book of poetry, *Laguna Woman*. Her work has appeared in many journals and magazines and is widely anthologized. She has received a MacArthur Foundation Grant and a Lila Wallace–Reader's Digest Foundation Writer's Fellowship. She lives in Tucson, Arizona.

LUCI TAPAHONSO is a member of the Navajo Nation. She was born and raised in Shiprock, New Mexico, and is currently an assistant professor of English at the University of Kansas in Lawrence, where she lives with her husband and children. She has published four books of poetry: *One More Shiprock Night*, *Seasonal Woman*, *A Breeze Swept Through*, and *Sáanii Dahataał, The Women Are Singing*. Her work has appeared in many journals and is widely anthologized.

DEBRA CALLINGTHUNDER was born in Lander, Wyoming, and has lived most of her life on the Wind River Indian Reservation. She is a member of the Northern Arapaho tribe but also shares Shoshone and Cheyenne blood. She is the former editor of a reservation weekly, the *Wind River News*; a regular columnist for the *Salt Lake Tribune*; and a reporter for the *Casper Star-Tribune*.

MARK TRAHANT was born in Fort Hall, Idaho, and is a member of the Shoshone-Bannock tribe. A journalist, Trahant was a finalist for the Pulitzer Prize for National Reporting in 1987 for a series in the *Arizona Republic* titled "Fraud in Indian Country," which also won the George Polk Award and Paul Tobekin Memorial Award from Columbia University. In 1985, he received a citation as Editor of the Year from the National Press Foundation for his work as editor of *Navajo Times Today*, a daily newspaper formerly published on the Navajo Reservation. He is currently executive news editor of the *Salt Lake Tribune* in Salt Lake City, Utah, where he lives with his wife and son.

WHITE DEER OF AUTUMN (GABRIEL HORN) has taught in reservation schools, American Indian Movement survival schools, public schools, and junior colleges. He is currently a teacher in Florida as well as a member of the National Committee on American Indian History. He serves as a wisdomkeeper on the Wisdomkeepers Council for Ki-tu-wah in Asheville, North Carolina. He was nominated for the Human Rights Award in Minnesota for his work to further Indian rights.

ELIZABETH WOODY was born in Ganado, Arizona, in 1959. She is of Wasco, Warm Springs, and Navajo descent and is an enrolled member of the Confederated Tribes of Warm Springs, Oregon. She studied creative writing at the Institute of American Indian Arts in Santa Fe and later graduated from The Evergreen State College in Olympia, Washington. Her writing has been published in numerous journals and anthologies, including the *Greenfield Review*, *Tyuonyi*, *Dancing on the Rim of the World*, *Talking Leaves*, and the forthcoming *Reinventing the Enemy's Language*. Her book of poetry, *Hand Into Stone*, received an American Book Award from the Before Columbus Foundation in 1990. She is a co-founder of the Northwest Native American Writers Association. She lives in Portland, Oregon.

PHOTOGRAPHERS

NANCY ACKERMAN, of Mohawk descent on her grandmother's side, is a photojournalist based outside Montreal, where she lives with her husband and two children. Her work has appeared in numerous publications, including the *Montreal Gazette*, *Toronto Star*, *London Times*, and *Newsweek*. She is currently at work on a book of portraits of First Nations women.

CHARLES AGEL, of Seneca descent, is currently working on a MFA in photography at the University of Buffalo in New York. His images have appeared in numerous newspapers and magazines, including *The Washington Post*, *Baltimore Sun*, *The New York Times*, and *Los Angeles Times*. He received an Award of Excellence in the Pictures of the Year Contest, Best Photographic Content Award from the Native Indian/Inuit Photographers Association, and several regional awards from the National Press Photographers Association.

KENNY BLACKBIRD, a member of the Assiniboine/Sioux tribes, grew up on the Fort Belknap Reservation in Montana. He recently completed a degree in photojournalism at the University of Montana and has worked with the National Geographic Society and Turner Publishing. His work has been published in *The New York Times*, *Dallas Morning News*, and *Insight Guide: Native America*. He is presently a staff photographer with *Indian Country Today* in Rapid City, South Dakota.

JOE MARTIN CANTRELL grew up in Tahlequah, Oklahoma, and is a member of the Cherokee Nation. His photography has been published in *Time*, *Newsweek*, *The New York Times*, and many other newspapers and magazines, as well as in numerous books, including *The Sultan of Brunei* and *Fractals: Patterns of Chaos*. His work has been shown at galleries and museums worldwide and is currently featured in a touring exhibition chronicling the emotional impact of the Vietnam War. He lives in Portland, Oregon, with his daughter.

DOROTHY CHOCOLATE, a member of the Rae Dogriv band of the Dene tribe, was born and raised around Rae Lakes in the Northwest Territories. She is currently a photo editor at the *Northern Star* in Yellowknife, Northwest Territories, where she lives with her family.

JESSE COODAY, a member of the Tlingit tribe, exhibits his work widely in the United States and abroad. His images have appeared in a number of publications, including *The Village Voice*, *The Washington Post*, and Lucy Lippard's *Mixed Blessings*. He lives and works in New York City.

ELTON DANIELS is a part-time photographer who specializes in documenting Native American life in the Southwest. He is a member of the Navajo Nation. He lives in Farmington, New Mexico.

GRAYWOLF was born in Jay, Oklahoma, in 1933 and is a member of the Cherokee Nation of Oklahoma. His photographs of Native American life and people have been shown at several exhibitions in the United States. He lives in New York City.

LARRY GUS, a member of the Hopi tribe, is a free-lance photographer based in Riverside, California. He attended the California Institute of the Arts and was later an exclusive free-lancer for the *Los Angeles Times*. He now shoots frequently for the Associated Press.

EUGENE JACK, a member of the Paiute tribe, was born and raised in Fallon, Nevada. A fire fighter for the U.S. Forest Service for some fifteen years, he is now a staff photographer at the *Nevada Appeal*. He also teaches photojournalism at the University of Nevada at Reno and Western Nevada Community College.

CARM LITTLE TURTLE, of Apache, Tarahumara, and Mexican descent, shows her work throughout the United States. She is also a poet, actress, and operating-room nurse. She and her husband divide their time between homes in New Mexico and Arizona.

LARRY MCNEIL, a member of the Tlingit/Nishka tribes, shows his work extensively in the United States and abroad. He is a professor of photography at the Institute of American Indian Arts and vice-president of the Native Indian/Inuit Photographers Association, which awarded him for outstanding outdoor photography and outstanding photographic technical quality in 1992. McNeil lives with his family in Santa Fe, New Mexico.

LEE MARMON was born and raised in Laguna, New Mexico, and has been photographing Laguna and Acoma pueblos since 1947. His images are widely published in books, newspapers, and magazines, including *Time*, *The New York Times Magazine*, *Saturday Evening Post*, and *Los Angeles Times*. He owns and manages the Blue-Eyed Indian Bookshop near Laguna Pueblo.

BERNICE MORRISON, a Beaver Village Inupiaq, was born and raised in Fairbanks, Alaska. Her work has been exhibited in Canada and the United States and has appeared in several publications, including *Canadian Women's Studies*, *Alaska Magazine*, and *Alaska Native News*. She is a member of the board of directors of the Native Indian/Inuit Photographers Association and is currently a student at the Institute of American Indian Arts in Santa Fe, New Mexico.

DAVID NEEL is a Canadian artist and photographer of Kwagiutl descent. He trained and worked as a photojournalist in the United States for several years and now lives in British Columbia. His work has been exhibited extensively, and his book, *Our Chiefs and Elders: Words and Photographs of Native Leaders*, was published in 1992.

CAMELA PAPPAN, of Ponca descent and a member of the Seneca Nation, grew up in Oklahoma. Her work has been exhibited at a one-woman show at the Native Indian/Inuit Photographers Association Gallery in Hamilton, Ontario, and at shows in Oklahoma and New Mexico. She is currently a student at the University of Oklahoma.

MARY ANNETTE PEMBER is a member of the Red Cliff Ojibwa tribe of Wisconsin. Her work has appeared in *Time*, *Life*, *Newsweek*, *The New York Times*, and many other publications, and she is currently a staff photographer with *The Oregonian* in Portland, Oregon. She has received several regional National Press Photographers Association awards, Best of Gannett awards, and other honors.

SHELDON PRESTON, a member of the Navajo Nation, is a former staff photographer with *Navajo Nation Today*. His images have appeared in *Native Peoples Magazine*, *Winds of Change*, and in a book, *Writing and Being*. He is currently studying architecture at Arizona State University in Tempe.

MONTY ROESSEL was born in Mesa, Arizona, in 1961 and is a member of the Navajo Nation. A former editor of *Navajo Nation Today*, his most recent work has appeared in magazines including *Arizona Highways*, *New Mexico Magazine*, *Native Peoples Magazine*, *The New York Times Magazine*, *GEO*, and *Sports Illustrated*, as well as in many books, including *Insight Guide: Native America* and *Beyond the Mythic West*. He is currently at work on a series of children's books about Native American cultures. He lives with his wife and four children in Kayenta, Arizona.

OWEN SEUMPTEWA, a member of the Hopi tribe, divides his time between homes on the Hopi Reservation and in Flagstaff, Arizona. A self-taught photographer, his work has appeared in a number of publications, including *Arizona Highways*, *Native Peoples Magazine*, and *The New York Times*, as well as in the book, *Four Views of Hopi*. He is currently an administrator with the Hopi Foundation in Kykotsmovi, Arizona, and lectures often on Native American culture and photography.

GREG STAATS, a member of the Mohawk Nation, was born and raised on the Six Nations Reserve. His work has appeared in publications including *Photo Life* and *Photography*, and he exhibits regularly in Canada, the United States, and abroad. He lives in Toronto, Ontario.

RICHARD RAY WHITMAN, a member of the Creek Nation, was born in 1949 in Claremore, Oklahoma. He exhibits his work extensively in galleries and museums in the United States and abroad.

PHOTOGRAPHY NOTES

Cover, upper right *Chief Richard Maracle, Mohawk. Six Nations Reserve, Ontario.* — Greg Staats

Cover, center *Uren Lenard, All-Idaho Indian Expo. Boise, Idaho.* — Kenny Blackbird.

Inside, *Rick Bartow, Yurok artist. South Beach, Oregon.* — Joe Martin Cantrell

4 *"Mystery Figure in Time Warp."* — Carm Little Turtle

7 *"Dalava." Ryan Seumptewa, Hopi.* — Owen Seumptewa

9 *"My Mother Married My Father Because She Said He Looked Like Elvis Presley."* — Camela Pappan

11 *Zeke (Cherokee) and Chick (Yakima) McConnell.* — Joe Martin Cantrell.

12 *"Young Warrior." West Delta Park Powwow. Portland, Oregon.* — Joe Martin Cantrell

13 *Rick Christie, Cherokee, West Delta Park Powwow. Portland, Oregon.* — Joe Martin Cantrell

14 *Eagle dancers. Laguna, New Mexico.* — Lee Marmon

15 *Rachelle Reuben, School #19. Buffalo, New York.* — Charles Agel

16 *Jim (Ojibwa), lead singer of Hate, Kill, Destroy, a Green Bay punk band, describes himself as a sensitive guy.* — Mary Annette Pember

17 *Levi Carson, All-Idaho Indian Expo. Boise, Idaho.* — Kenny Blackbird

18 *Mary Des Rosier, Blackfeet physician, at her family's cabin on the Blackfeet Reservation, Montana.* — Kenny Blackbird

19 Top: *Marlin Thompson, leader of "the Tribe," a group of Native American inmates. Nevada State Prison, Carson City, Nevada.* — Eugene Jack

19 Bottom: *Doug George. Akwesasne Reserve, Quebec.* — Larry Gus

21 *Uren Lenard, All-Idaho Indian Expo. Boise, Idaho.* — Kenny Blackbird

22 Top/bottom: *A Hopi marine undergoes a cleansing ceremony after returning from Kuwait. Bacavi, Hopi Reservation, Arizona.* — Larry Gus

23 Top: *Tony Nieto, Apache. Riverside, California.* Bottom: *Alice Pioche, Navajo. Near Farmington, New Mexico.* — Larry Gus

24 *Protesting Navajo relocation. Dinnebito, Arizona.* — Larry Gus

25 *"Abandoned Technology." Moenave, Navajo Reservation, Arizona.* — Sheldon Preston

26 *Chinle Chapter House. Chinle, Navajo Reservation, Arizona.* — Larry Gus

27 *A member of the last graduating class of the Phoenix Indian School. Phoenix, Arizona.* — Monty Roessel

28 *Chief Joe Mathias, Squamish. Vancouver, British Columbia. From Our Chiefs and Elders: Words and Photographs of Native Leaders. Courtesy of UBC Press, Vancouver, British Columbia.* — David Neel

29 Top: *A Canadian official searches a car on the border of Akwesasne Reserve in Ontario and Quebec and the St. Regis Reservation in New York.* — Larry Gus

29 Bottom: *Former Navajo-Hopi Joint Use Area. Big Mountain, Arizona.* — Graywolf

30 *Protesting Navajo relocation. Hard Rock, Arizona.* — Monty Roessel

31 *"Hopi Clown Boy."* — Owen Seumptewa

32 *Mike Smith, honor guard, North American Indian Days. Browning, Montana.* — Kenny Blackbird

33 *Traditional dancer, Milk River Indian Days. Fort Belknap Reservation, Montana.* — Kenny Blackbird

34 *"Imaginary Pueblo." Movie set for The Dark Wind. Moenave, Navajo Reservation, Arizona.* — Sheldon Preston

35 *Pearl Nakai. Red Valley, Navajo Reservation, Arizona.* — Monty Roessel

36 *Dinetah petroglyphs in northwest New Mexico symbolizing the Navajo hero twins, Monster Slayer and Child Born For Water.* — Monty Roessel

37 *Ruth Roessel teaches her granddaughter, Jaclyn Roessel, traditional Navajo weaving. Round Rock, Navajo Reservation, Arizona.* — Monty Roessel

38 *"A Beginning." Grand River Powwow. Six Nations Reserve, Ontario.* — Greg Staats

39 *Navajo great-grandmother. Shiprock, New Mexico.* — Monty Roessel

40 *Silas Quluat, Inuit, remains at fishing camp while his father hunts walrus. Near Igloolik, Northwest Territories.* — Nancy Ackerman

41 *Inuit children play on the roofs of fishing huts on the shore of the Arctic Ocean. Igloolik, Northwest Territories.* — Nancy Ackerman

42 *Main street of Igloolik, Northwest Territories.* — Nancy Ackerman

43 *Silas Quluat, Inuit, heads toward fishing camp near Igloolik, Northwest Territories.* — Nancy Ackerman

44 *Dinetah petroglyphs. Northwest New Mexico.* — Monty Roessel

45 *Mary Montoure, Mohawk. Six Nations Reserve, Ontario.* — Greg Staats

46 *Michel and Mary Pasteen, Innu elders. Sheshatshit Reserve, Newfoundland.* — Nancy Ackerman

47 *"La Belle Sauvage."* — Camela Pappan

48 *Buffalo dancers. Laguna, New Mexico.* — Lee Marmon

49 *Plains Indian Museum Powwow. Cody, Wyoming.* — Kenny Blackbird

50 *Eagle staff, All-Idaho Indian Expo. Boise, Idaho.* — Kenny Blackbird

51 *"Abandoned Shelter." Near Cow Springs, Navajo Reservation, Arizona.* — Sheldon Preston

52 *Center pole of sun dance lodge. Rocky Boys Reservation, Montana.* — Kenny Blackbird

53 *"She Who Knows." Theda Brant, Mohawk, Grand River Powwow. Six Nations Reserve, Ontario.* — Greg Staats

54 *"Forward Movement." Grand River Powwow, Six Nations Reserve, Ontario.* — Greg Staats

55 *Mona Stonefish and her son, Karontose Jacobs (Mohawk/Delaware), Grand River Powwow. Six Nations Reserve, Ontario.* — Greg Staats

56 *Fred Elliot (Mohawk), traditional dancer. Grand River Powwow. Six Nations Reserve, Ontario.* — Greg Staats

ACKNOWLEDGMENTS

I would like to thank Yvonne Maracle and Carol Hill at the Native Indian/Inuit Photographers Association and Gloria Lomahaftewa and Margaret Archuleta at the Heard Museum for helping to locate photographers. The Native American Journalists Association and the Wheelwright Museum also suggested several photographers. A special word of gratitude is due to Monty Roessel, whose keen eye and sound counsel sharpened my thinking about this project. Thanks also to Cindy Black and Richard Cohn at Beyond Words Publishing; to Julie Livingston, whose comments on the text were smart and insightful; to Jim Lommasson and Mary Ann W. Puls, whose design brought coherence and style to a wide variety of material; and to Chris Landon, for his cultural expertise. Most important, I wish to thank the writers, photographers, and their subjects for allowing us to share a part of their lives and cultures. Without their patience, kindness, and generosity, this book would not have been possible.

—John Gattuso